BREAKING
THE
WALLS
OF
LIMITATION

by
Jonathan B. Fisher

THIS BOOK IS DEDICATED TO:

My Mother and Father in loving memory
Sarah A. Lighty
Ralph A. Fisher

My second Mother
Louise Lighty

My Grandfather
Clyde Lighty

The Future Generation
Malcolm Johnson
Maya Johnson
Imani Hughley
Trey Blackman
Shannon Ellision
Shantel Ellision
Lil' Shawn Lighty
Natalie Soley
Elijah Robinson
Lil' Andre Robinson
Emily Long

TABLE OF CONTENTS

Part II

Acknowledgements

I would like to thank:

My entire family
Michelle Clancy and the Clancy family
Pastor Eric and Lisa Johnson
Pastor Joe and Frances Parker & Wayside Baptist
    Church
    (I'll never forget where I started)
Bishop Bernard Jordan and Zoe Ministries
The Long family
The Stuyvesant crew
    (Karin, Mina, Shawn, Samantha, Quanya,
    Billy, Rose, Steve)
The Holmes Family

Grandma and Pop and
    C.P. Bryant
Dave Young
Pastor Michael Gray
Pastor John Credle
Pastor Peterson
Vincent Coleman
Susu and Niki
Arvin "Slik" Stevens
Kyle McBridge
(Barbershop) T.J.
Aunt Gwen and Family
John Tillery
Carl Webber
Martin Christie
Joseph Salyes

My Brothers for Life, King David Lodge #7

Preface

I can say that 2002 was one
of the best years of my life.
I can truly say that I came
out of darkness and into the
light. I found truth which
has set me free. Many think
that they have truth, but no
one can give you truth; you
have to seek and find it. I
think that the most important
chapter in this book is "What
Lies Beneath." That is the
only thing that matters,
because that's where the
truth is. America, open your
eyes. The Bible says watch as
well as pray. It's okay to
pray, but don't forget to
watch. Everybody is waiting

for Jesus to come back, but
before he does, there are a
lot of things we are going to
see and partake of.

We are living in a time
when the parents have become
children and the children
have become parents. The
child tells the parents what
they are or are not going to
do. They go and come as they
please. They have no respect
for themselves or anybody
else, and they know
everything. You can't tell
them anything. Parents go to
work and work hard every day
to put food on the table and
a roof over their children's
heads, and the child in
return gives them his behind
to kiss. These are the times
we live in. Some parents have
the nerve to buy the child

one hundred dollar sneakers
and designer clothes. I
wouldn't buy anything. They
would wear the same thing all
year round. I want to ask you
a question? Are you the
parent or the child? The
government wants to tell you
how to raise your child, but
they won't help you take care
of them. I believe in the
word of God. If you spare the
rod, you spoil the child. You
don't have to abuse the
child, but you should have
order and respect.

In this time in which we
live, boyfriends and
girlfriends stay together
longer than husbands and
wives. I think many of us
marry for the wrong reasons.
We don't think logically; our
moves are based on our

feelings and emotions. I have noticed that a lot of women want a wedding but not a marriage. They plan out the wedding so wonderfully. They have everything together ready to go. I think they should have sat down and planned the marriage, just like they planned the wedding. The outcome would be great. Do you want a wedding or a marriage? A wedding is a ceremony that lasts for a couple of hours. A marriage is for a lifetime. I see now that sickness and health are very important in this day and time.

I believe that a lot of people are sick because of their belief patterns. Disease is nothing more than a thought in you that has

come to a level of dis-ease.
Cancer is nothing more than a
thought in you that can't
serve, cancer. I have noticed
that life moves in cycles.
There is a cycle for
everything. Do you know that
every fifty-two days your
life goes through a cycle?
There are seven fifty-two day
cycles in a year. Everything
in life revolves around
numbers; God geometrizes.

If there was one thing I
would tell the world right
now it would be to get some
money and put it away. Now is
the time. There are some
things are about to unfold,
and the body of Christ needs
to have some money. The Bible
says money is a defense (look
at O.J. Simpson). A lot of
people have a problem with

preachers talking about money. You need to start getting your barns filled with plenty of money. I watch how church people (not the world people) have criticized people like Rev. Ike, Creflo Dollar, Leroy Thompson, and Bishop E. Bernard Jordan. But the day is coming when those church people are going to wish they had taken heed and listened. If you need to get your finances straight and your barns filled with plenty of money, those are the people that you contact A.S.A.P. He that has an ear, let him hear. This is a do or die time we live in. We can't sit down and wait for things to happen. We have to make things happen. "Choose ye this day life or death." Don't wait for your friends,

mother, father, church, or
family. Everybody is held
accountable for themselves.
Your time is not long, so
make the most of life now. As
above so beneath; as within
so without. This is why we
need to break down the walls
of limitation. This is only
food for thought.

> The world is ready to give up
> its secrets if we only know how
> to knock, how to give it the
> necessary blow. There is not
> limit to the power of the human
> mind.
>   --Swami Vivekananda

PART I

Our lives begin to end the day we
become silent about things that
matter.
>   --Martin Luther King, Jr.

My philosophy is that not only are
you responsible
for your life, but doing the best at
this moment puts you in the best
place for the moment.
>   --Oprah Winfrey

People might not get all they work
for in this world, but they must
certainly work for all they get.
>   --Frederick Douglass

Opportunity is missed by most people
because it is dressed in overalls
and looks like work.
>   --Thomas A. Edison

Do not go where the path may lead,
go instead where there is no path
and leave a trail.
>   --Ralph Waldo Emerson

IT'S NOT OVER YET, YOU'RE CHOSEN

We are troubled on every
side, yet not distressed;
We are perplexed, but not
in despair; Persecuted, but
not forsaken; Cast down,
but not destroyed.
    --2 Corinthians 4:8-9 (KJV)

Ye have not chosen me, but
I have chosen you, and
ordained you, that ye
should go and bring forth
fruit, and that your fruit
should remain; that
whatever ye shall ask of
the father in my name, he
may give it to you.
          --John 15:16 (KJV)

Whatever you have gone
through in the past or are
going through now, I want you

to know your life isn't over
yet. You may not be able to
help where you've been, but
you can sure help where
you're going. Listen to me;
never let your situation lock
you in. There is always a way
out. I repeat, there is
always a way out. The problem
we are having is that many of
us don't know there is a way
out because we are so caught
up in the situation that we
can't see our way out. If you
are at this moment in a
difficult situation, take
your eyes off of your present
situation and start seeing
yourself overcoming that
situation.

From this day forth, stop
letting your circumstances
keep you from living.
Whatever you do, please!

Don't worry. This is, I
believe, the reason why a lot
of us are in the position
we're in. Worrying is the
worse thing anybody can do.
Look at this:

> Therefore I tell you, do
> not worry about your life,
> what you will eat or drink;
> or about your body, what
> you will wear. Is not life
> more important than food,
> and the body more important
> than clothes?
> >   --Matthew 6:25 (NIV)

> Who of you by worrying can
> add a single hour to his
> life?
> >   --Matthew 6:28 (NIV)

You can worry all you want
to, but you can't change
anything. What sense does it
make to get yourself all

stressed out and upset over nothing? All the energy you put into worrying should be put in faith. Let's look at this. It was Bishop E. Bernard Jordan that brought this revelation of the Scripture to my attention.

For the pagans (Gentiles) run after all these things, and your heavenly father knows that you need them. The Gentiles were known as the worldly people. What do people in the world want? They want houses, cars, clothes, luxurious lifestyle, and lots of money. That is what the world runs after, and your heavenly father knows that you have need of these things. These same things the world runs after.

But seek first his kingdom
and his righteousness, and
all these things will be
given to you as well. To
seek first God's kingdom is
to seek his order of
operation. His laws,
precepts, and will. And all
these things will be given
to you. (House, car,
clothes, luxurious
lifestyle, and money.)
            --Matthew 6:33 (NIV)

God has chosen you. Yes
you. You were created for a
purpose. You are not a
mistake. You are a miracle.
Look at this:

For I know the plans I have
for you, declares the Lord,
plans to prosper you and
not to harm you. Plans to
give you hope and a future.
            --Jeremiah 29:11 (NIV)

God has a plan and a purpose for you. He has tailor made your life. It's up to you to put it on and walk in it.

> Before I formed you in the womb I knew you; before you were born I set you apart; I appointed you as a prophet to the nations.
> --Jeremiah 1:5 (NIV)

You may be asking yourself this question. If I'm chosen, then why am I going through what I'm going through? When you come into the realization about God's plan for your life, you focus on his will for your life. The ups and downs of life don't really affect you because you know you are God's chosen. You are

still alive. Life's ups and
downs don't kill you. They
will only make you stronger.
Only the strong survive.
Don't let fear lock you up.
Fear is False Evidence
Appearing Real. Be careful at
whom you point your finger.
You can't blame the devil for
everything. The devil doesn't
make you do anything. You are
responsible for your own
actions. You may be your own
devil. You are God's
creation. You will never find
God until you find yourself.
And you will never find
yourself until you find God.

THE AUTHORITY OF ADVANCEMENT

Then God said let us make man in our image, in our likeness, and let them rule over the fish of the sea and the birds of the air, and over all the creatures that move along the ground.

God blessed them and said to them be fruitful and increase in number, fill the earth and subdue it. Rule over the fish of the sea and the birds of the air and over every living creature that moves on the ground.
                    --Genesis 1:26, 28 (NIV)

God has given you the authority to advance. Your life is not supposed to be in idle. God is a God of movement. God wants you to go higher and higher. It makes no sense for you to serve a God for twenty years and still be in the same circumstance twenty years later. Something is wrong. If God is so great and able to do all things but fails, then why haven't you advanced? It's obvious that you're doing something wrong.

God's word doesn't lie. The problem is that you haven't taken your authority to advance. You should be at a much higher level now than you were last year, and you should be at a much higher level next year than you're at now. Your authority to advance is for every element of your life. You should advance in your finances, family, marriage, business, and the church. The more you walk in your authority, the stronger you will get. Even when the storm winds of life blow, they won't affect you because your authority is so powerful. Nothing can stop you from advancing. The only person who can stop you is you. Set goals for yourself. If you fail to plan, you plan to fail. Where do you see yourself in the next five years? What area in your life do you want to advance in? You cannot change the world until you change yourself. You were created to advance. Start walking in it and put all things under your feet. God is calling for those people who are not afraid to advance. Are you ready?

WHAT IS LIFE?

The thief cometh not, but
for to steal, and to kill,
and to destroy. I am come
that they might have life,
and that they might have it
more abundantly.
                    --John 10:10 (KJV)
Man that is born of a woman
is of few days, and full of
trouble.
                    --Job 14:1 (KJV)

Is life just going to work,
coming home, watching TV, and
going to bed? This routine
continues every day; is this
life? There is no fun in
this. This doesn't sound like
an abundant life to me. Life
is supposed to be fun, happy,
joyful, and pleasant. It's
not supposed to be hard,
stressful, unpleasant, and
depressing. Life is not

working to pay bills. Let me let you in on a little secret; you will always have bills even when you're dead and gone. Your life is to enjoy. When was the last time you went on a vacation? When was the last time you went to a Broadway play or out to the movies? Enjoy your life; don't let your life live you.

Most people can't enjoy life because they are worrying about this and about that. One thing I noticed in the church is that everybody is waiting. Waiting for what? Nothing is going to happen until you get up off your behind and go and get what you want out of life. Jesus said, "I come that you might have life and that you might have it more abundantly." The

key word here is "might."
According to your faith, so
be it. If you want it, go and
get it. I learned a long time
ago that destiny is not a
matter of chance. It's a
matter of choice. I don't
believe in good luck or bad
luck. Some people say, "Maybe
this is the kind of life God
wants me to live." "God has
favorites, but I'm not one of
them." This kind of mind set
is a wall of limitation. God
is a respecter of principles,
not persons. I don't care if
your father was the president
of the United States. God
will not show you more
favoritism over anybody else.
If you do and follow the
principles in God's word, you
will see that your life
doesn't have anything to do
with who your father was or

where you came from. Stop
making excuses. When I was
growing up, I was poor. I
didn't have this, and I
didn't have that. Start
finding solutions.

Anytime somebody asks you a
question, the first thing
that comes out of your mouth
is, I can't do this or I
can't do that. There is
another thing I want to look
at, and then I'll leave you
alone. If you want an
abundant life, you can't have
an "I'm trying" spirit.
Someone asks you, "Are you
coming to Bible study
tonight?" "Oh, I don't know.
I'm gonna try to come." Right
there that person knows they
are not going. People are
always trying to do
something. Just do it. Don't

try. Either you're going to Bible study or you're not. You can't try to have an abundant life. Either you will or you won't. Jesus never tried anything; he just did it. He didn't try to heal the sick. He didn't try to give sight to the blind. He didn't try to die for me and you; he did it. I didn't try to write this book; I did it. Just do it. You will be amazed at how many things you get done with a "just do it" attitude. Your life will never be the same. Enjoy your life to the fullest. You can have, be, and do whatever you want in life. Remember to always walk in your authority to advance and live your abundant life.

YOUR FUTURE IS IN YOUR MOUTH

> The tongue has the power of life and death, and those who love it will eat its fruit.
>
> --Proverbs 18:21 (NIV)

> A man shall be satisfied with good by the fruit of his mouth; and the recompense of a man's hands shall be rendered unto him.
>
> --Proverbs 12:14 (KJV)

What you say is what you get. The problem that many have is they don't know how powerful their words are. I remember when I was little, we used to sing a song: "Sticks and stones may break my bones, but words will never hurt me." That was a lie because words do hurt. I would rather be hurt physically than to be hurt by words. Your words form and shape your world. Look at this:

> Thou shalt also decree a thing, and it shall be established unto thee: and the light shall shine upon thy ways.
> --Job 22:28 (KJV)

If you have been saying negative things, then that's why negative things appear in your world. If you are saying how you are always broke, and you are never going to get out of debt, then that's what is going to happen. Start saying things that you want to see happen. Speak positively and positive things will start happening.

Whatever you want to see, start calling it into manifestation. The more you practice, the better the results.

> For verily I say unto you, whosoever shall say unto this mountain, be thou removed, and be though cast into the sea; and shall not doubt in his heart, but shall believe that those things which he saith shall come to pass, he shall have whatever he saith.

You create your own reality by the words you speak. You have the power to move problems out of your life. You also have the power to call abundance, prosperity, success, and increase into your life. It works if you work it. Start speaking to your mountains and watch the outcome.

THE SECRET OF PRAYER

> Therefore, I say unto you, whatever things ye desire, when ye pray, believe that ye receive them, and ye shall have them.
> --Mark 11:24 (KJV)

I have realized that when people go to God in prayer, most of the time they are telling God about their problems, wants, and desires. Then they sit back, wait for God to do what they ask of him. God knows about your problems, wants, and desires. When you go to God in prayer, don't go to him complaining. Go to him rejoicing. You know why you don't get what you prayed for? Because you don't believe. The Bible says, "Believe that ye receive them, and ye shall have them." Even if you don't see it with your physical eyes, you have to believe it. So basically the secret of prayer is convincing yourself that you already have what you're praying for. If you are praying for a financial breakthrough, believe that you have it and you will receive it. The just shall live by faith. I know some people may say it's hard to believe in something that you can't touch or see physically. That's why it's very important that we as Christians walk by faith.

> Now faith is the substance of
> things hoped for, the
> evidence of things not seen.
> --Hebrews 11:1 (KJV)

Faith is the most powerful
weapon we have. In fact, the
Bible declares in Hebrews
11:6 that without faith it is
impossible to please him.
Faith is the foundation that
we need to accomplish any
task that is presented before
us. I don't think there is
anything better than having
your prayers answered. The
answer is inside you. I
notice that a lot of people
look up at the sky to pray
and talk to God. The Bible
says, "Greater is he that is
in you than he that's in the
world." So that means when
you pray, you should look
within and not up. Everything

you need is within you. If
you fail to look within, you
learn to live without.

POVERTY DOESN'T LIVE HERE ANYMORE

For you are becoming
progressively acquainted
with and recognizing more
strongly and clearly the
grace of Lord Jesus Christ
(his kindness, his gracious
generosity, his undeserved
favor and spiritual
blessing), [in] that though
he was [so very] rich, in
order that by his poverty
you might become enriched
(abundantly supplied).
   --2 Corinthians 8:9 (AMP)

Poverty should not be
living in your world. If it
is, that means you are still

living within the walls of
limitation. Poverty is a
consciousness, and too many
people have it. There are two
sides to every coin. So the
other side of poverty would
be prosperity. Just like the
other side of fear is faith.
God wants the best for his
children. Look at this.

> Beloved, I pray that you
> may prosper in every way
> and [that your body] may
> keep well, even as [I know]
> your soul keeps well and
> prospers.
>   --John 1:2 (AMP)

Prosperity is not just
money, but it is good health
and well being. Let's talk
about money. Ecclesiastes
10:19 says, "Money answers
all things." I notice that

people who have a lot of money have a lot of answers. People who don't have a lot of money have a lot of questions. Which one are you? I have also noticed that people in church don't like to talk about money unless they are on the receiving end. Money talks in the world system. So in order to operate and be effective in the world, you have to have some money. Your job is not where your money comes from. The money you get from your job is seed money. You plant it. Just because you make $50,000 a year doesn't mean that's all the money you can make that year. Man determines your salary. God determines your income. God will cause money to come to you from many different places. Believe it or not, but people who don't like preachers who talk about money, nine times out of ten don't have money. Getting money is nothing. What will you do with it when you get it? In the Bible there are a lot of scriptures that talk about money, but the Bible speaks highly about wealth. Look at this:

> But you shall (earnestly) remember the Lord your God, for it is he who gives you power to get wealth, that he may establish his covenant which he swore to your father, as it is this day.
> --Deuteronomy 8:18 (AMP)

God never said he would give you wealth. He said he would give you the power to get wealth. Having money and being wealthy are two different things. You could receive a ten million dollar inheritance and people would say he or she is rich. But if you took that ten million dollars and turned it into one hundred million dollars, you would be wealthy. Wealth is the ability to create money. Since God has given us the power to get wealth, we know God has empowered us to create money. Let me tell you right now, you are rich and prosperous. You have to start walking around in that consciousness. You need to see yourself as God sees you. God sees you as rich, prosperous, healthy, and blessed, not broke, busted, and disgusted. If you are reading this book right now

and you don't have any money
in your pocket or in your
bank account, you're still
rich. You have to use your
third eye (MIND'S EYE) and
visualize your pockets filled
with money and your bank
account filled with money.
See yourself wearing the
nicest clothes, living in the
nicest house, driving the
nicest car. You have to walk
by faith, not by sight. You
have to believe it is so,
even if your present
circumstance says it is not
so. You need to make what I
call a "manifestation list."
Take out a piece of paper and
write down all your desires
and number them. A lot of
people don't realize it but
there is power in writing
things down. The Bible says
write the vision. Anytime

people are getting ready to
make a business deal, they
say "get it in writing."
After you have written down
all of your desires, write at
the bottom of the list, "God
is the source of my supply.
God's provision flows freely,
and unlimitedly in my life.
Every desire on my list God
has already manifested it. I
give God all the praise,
glory, and honor." Every
morning and every night,
meditate on your
manifestation list. Cross off
your desires as they come
into manifestation. Remember,
according to your faith, so
be it.

WHAT LIES BENEATH

For everyone who comes to me and listens to my words [in order to heed their teaching] and does them, I will show you what he is like:

He is like a man building a house, who dug and went down deep and laid a foundation upon the rock; and when a flood arose, the torrent broke against that house and could not shake or move it, because it had been securely built or founded on a rock.

But he who merely hears and does not practice doing my words is like a man who built a house on the ground without a foundation, against which the torrent

burst, and immediately it
collapsed and fell and the
breaking and ruin of that
house was great.
    --Luke 6:47-49 (Amplified)

Do you focus on the outward
appearance or the inward
appearance? I realize that it
doesn't matter how big your
house is. It doesn't matter
what kind of car you drive or
what kind of clothes you
wear. I found out that people
who look happy really are not
always happy. Those marriages
that seem free of problems
really aren't that way. The
only thing that matters is
what lies beneath. Ask
yourself this question: "What
lies beneath my life? What is
my life built on?"

Everything in your life is built on something. Your job, marriage, family, finances, children are all built on something. Life will send some storms your way, and whatever foundation you have built on will be tested in the storm. I don't know what kind of foundation you have built on, but let me show you what foundation you are supposed to build on:

According to the grace (the special endowment for my task) of God bestowed on me, like a skillful architect and master builder, I laid [the] foundation, and now another [man] is building upon it. But let each [man] be careful how he builds upon it. For no other foundation can anyone lay than that

which is [already] laid,
which is Jesus Christ (the
messiah, the anointed one).
But if anyone builds upon
the foundation, whether it
be with gold, silver,
precious stones, wood, hay,
straw, the work of each
[one] will become [plainly,
openly] I know [shown for
what it is]; for the day
[of Christ] will disclose
and declare it, because it
will be revealed with fire,
and the fire will test and
critically appraise the
character and worth of the
work each person has done.
        --I Corinthians 3:10-13
                    (Amplified)

In verse 11 we can see that
Jesus Christ is the
foundation. If you are not
building on Jesus Christ, you
are the man whose house fell

down after the storm came. Not only is it important to build your marriage, family, job, children, and finance on Jesus Christ, but how you build it is just as important. Once you have laid the foundation, how are you going to build? Look at verse 12. Are you going to use gold, silver, and precious stones, or are you going to use wood, hay, or straw? Some people like to do things their way. They don't follow God's word. These are the people who know everything. You can't tell them anything. They use wood, hay, and straw. When their work is tried by the fire, it burns up because they did it their way. Then there are those who follow God's word. They are like David going after God's own heart. These are the ones who use gold, silver, and precious stones. When it is tried by the fire, it stands because they followed the word of God. (Man does not live by bread alone, but by every word that comes from the mouth of God). You will never be able to live by every word that proceeds out of the mouth of God until you find the mouth of God. Which one are you? Do you use wood, hay, and straw or do you use gold, silver, and precious stones? Don't hold on to the outward appearance. Look at the inward appearance.

There is an old saying that says you can't judge a book by its cover. That is so true. The only way you can see something for what it really is, is to know what lies beneath. If your marriage, job, family, children, and finances are not doing so well, look at what lies beneath, lay the foundation and start building.

GET PLANTED

> And he shall be like a tree planted by the rivers of water, that bringeth forth its fruit in its season; its leaf also shall not wither, and whatsoever he doeth shall prosper.
> --Psalms 1:3

> For he shall be like a tree planted by the waters that spreads out its roots by the river; and it shall not see and fear when heat comes, but its leaf shall

be green. It shall not be
anxious and full of care in
the year of drought, nor
shall it cease yielding
fruit.
--Jeremiah 17:8 (AMP)

One of the most important
things we need to do as a
Christian is to get planted
in the word of God. It's not
enough just to quote
scriptures and memorize them.
You need to allow them to
become a part of you. A
farmer doesn't just talk
about his crops; he actually
plants seeds so that the
crops he was talking about
will become a reality. I know
people who quote scriptures
and talk about the Bible all
day long, but they are not
planted. Everybody is planted
in something. Some are planted
in the wrong thing. Some are

planted in the word of the God.
Look at this:

> Wherefore, by their fruits
> ye shall know them.
> --Matthew 12:33

What kinds of fruits does
your tree bear? You get
planted by meditating on the
word of God. You need to get
in the word and stay there.
When you get planted in the
word of God, your life will
never be the same. I think
one of the best experiences
you can have is when your
fruit comes forth in your
season as a result of being
planted in the word of God.
Your leaf will not wither.
Even when things don't seem
to be going your way and it
seems that everything is at a
standstill, you don't need to

worry. Your life will not wither away because you're planted. The only life you can have is a life in God. Whatever you do, don't get separated from God. Stand strong in faith and declare, as Paul did:

> For I am persuaded beyond doubt (am sure) that neither death nor life nor angels nor principalities, not things impending and threatening nor things to come, nor powers. Nor height nor depth nor anything else in all creation will be able to separate us from the love of God which is in Christ Jesus our Lord.
>
> --Rom. 8:38-39 (AMP)

TAKE OFF YOUR MASK

Do not lie to one another,
for you have stripped off
the old (unregenerate) self
with its evil practices.And
have clothed yourselves
with the new [spiritual
self], which is [ever in
the process of Being]
renewed and remolded into
[fuller and more perfect
knowledge upon] knowledge
after the image (the
likeness) of him who
created it.
  --Colossians 3:9-10 (AMP)

Therefore if any person is
[ingratified] in Christ
(the messiah), he is a new
creation (a new creature
altogether). The old
[previous moral and
spiritual condition] has

passed away. Behold, the
fresh and new has come.
--2 Corinthians 5:17 (AMP)

It is a proven fact that
people in the church wear
masks. They try to be people
they're not. They are still
the same old people but with
masks on. You can't hide who
you really are.

When you hide you hurt no
one but yourself. People walk
around having a form of
godliness denying the power
thereof. If you have taken
off the old man and put on
the new man, believe me you
don't have to tell anybody.
You should know a tree by
the fruit it bears. Nobody is
perfect, but we are all
striving for perfection.
Could it be that you have not

taken off the old man? You cannot put old wine in a new bottle. He who the son sets free is free indeed. Take off your mask. You're not fooling anybody. Some of us have been wearing a mask for so long we forgot who we really are. God is calling forth people who are real, not fake. You cannot walk in your destiny and be who God created you to be by wearing a mask. Be very careful because God will expose you. People will see the real you. Don't play with God!

BREAKING THE WALLS OF LIMITATION

> For as he thinketh in his heart so is he.
>> --Proverbs 23:7

I believe that we build our own wall of limitation. The way you think determines the way you live. Let's look at the word limitation. Limitation mean to confine or restrict. Do you feel confined or restricted? If you feel that way, keep reading: There are only two kinds of people on earth: volunteers and victims. Anybody from age 1-18 is a victim because they're still under their parents' guidance. Those that are 18 and over are volunteers because any issue they have in life, they signed up for it. In life some people deal with poverty, depression, lack, sickness, and low self-esteem. These are walls of limitation. People who deal with these things ordered them in their life. Somebody might say I never ordered sickness and lack in my life. I'm sorry to tell you this, but you order it because you paid attention to it. Whatever you pay attention to you will get.

If you don't like what's in your life, then don't pay attention to it. In order to change your life, you have to change your mind set.

Let this mind be in you, which was also in Christ Jesus.

--Philippians 2:5

Your mind is very powerful.
You may not realize it, but
everything you do starts in
the mind. Deciding what
you're going to wear, what
you're going to eat, or where
you're going to go starts in
your mind.

Let's look at the mind.
There are two distinct parts
of the mind: the conscious
and subconscious mind. The
conscious mind is like a
navigator or captain at the
front of the ship. The
subconscious is like the
people who work in the engine
room that take orders from
the captain (conscious). You
think with your conscious
mind and your subconscious
mind follows through. Once

the subconscious mind accepts a thought, it begins to bring it into manifestation. You must control your thoughts. Don't let your thoughts wander. Believe it or not, your thoughts have wings.

> Curse not the king, no, not even in your thoughts, and curse not the rich in your bedchamber, for a bird of the air will carry the voice, and a winged creature will tell the matter.
> --Ecclesiastes 10:20 (AMP)

Do you know that your thoughts travel 186,000 miles per second and 930,000 times faster than the sound of your voice? I know that all of this may seem a bit strange to some, but the truth will set you free.

You break your walls of limitation by changing your thought pattern. I have noticed that many people have a paper plate mentality. You know people who call themselves "children of the king." They eat on paper plates while they have their good china in the closet. You should eat on the good china all the time. I have seen people wear their best clothes only on special occasions. You should wear your best all the time. You shouldn't shop at the low budget department store. You should shop at the luxury stores.

You are a joint heir with Christ; you should be the best, live the best, eat the best, and wear the best. We are not our best because we have not made up our mind to be the best.

Your mind is a magnet. Whatever your mind focuses on, it draws that thing to it. Have you ever thought about somebody and that same person calls you out of the blue? If you focus your mind on prosperity, you magnetize it and draw it to you. The way you think and feel must be along the same lines. The way you think is not enough. The way you feel is important as well. Feeling is thought at its deepest level. I may think about prosperity, but if I don't feel prosperous, prosperity won't show up. Thought and feeling together are what magnetizes your wish.

You can have, be, and do whatever you want. The first thing you need to do is make up your mind; decide on what it is you want. Second, start off with your faith and believe. Third, visualize what you want (what you see is what you get). Fourth, feel it. Know that the God in you is bringing forth the thing you desire. Please remember a mind is a terrible thing to waste.

Life is like a movie: if you don't like the way your life is going, rewrite the screenplay of your life. I look at life as a game. If you understand the rules, you will be a winner. You are responsible for your life.

Live it to the fullest. Live
your life the way you want
to. Don't let the world's
circumstance dictate to you
how to live. What are you
going to do with your life?

> Man who is born of a woman
> is of few days and full of
> trouble.
>   --Job 14:1 (AMP)

No one can break the wall
of limitation but you. Can't
you see the walls coming
down? This is the day that
the Lord has made, rejoice
and be glad in it.

IT'S ON THE INSIDE

Lord, where is my peace
Where is my comfort
Where is my love
Where is my joy

IT'S ON THE INSIDE

Where is my power
Where is my wisdom
Where is my safety
Where is my victory

IT'S ON THE INSIDE

Where is my prosperity
Where is my success
Where is my wealth
Where is my health
      Look within

IT'S ON THE INSIDE

DON'T LET GO

My life is in a weak state
Everyday is harder and harder
When will the morning come
When is the sun going to
  shine

DON'T LET GO

The grip on my life is
  slipping
Problems come from many ways
I see no increase but
  decrease
The pain is hard to bear

DON'T LET GO

The storms are coming strong
Is there a shelter
Everybody has left me
I'm all alone
DON'T LET GO

WHO CAN STOP ME

There are many walls in front
  of me
So high and so wide
I hear laughing echoes from
  inside.

WHO CAN STOP ME

My enemies plot to destroy me
Traps are set before me
My so-called friends
Stand behind me

WHO CAN STOP ME

Hold my hands
Cover my mouth
Hold my feet
Cover my eyes

WHO CAN STOP ME

LET THERE BE LIGHT

I can't see in front of me
I can't see behind me
I can't see on my left side
I can't see on my right side
I can't see above me
I can't see below me

LET THERE BE LIGHT

I can't move
I can't think
I can't see myself

LET THERE BE LIGHT

Where is everybody
I call out but there is no
    answer
Where is the earth
Where am I

LET THERE BE LIGHT

GOOD MORNING

I cried all night long
Singing that same old song
Still feeling cloudy and grey
Hoping this might be my day
I can't wait to feel the
   sunrays

GOOD MORNING

Now I can dry my eyes
I can face my fears
It's time to cast my cares
My joy has just arrived

GOOD MORNING

PART II

Imagination is more important
than knowledge.
> --Albert Einstein

A wise man will make more
opportunities than he finds.
> --Sir Francis Bacon

We cannot always build the
future for our youth, but we can
build our youth for the future.
> --Franklin D. Roosevelt

Beware when the great God lets
loose a thinker on this planet.
> --Ralph Waldo Emerson

Life consists not in holding
good cards, but in playing those
you hold well.
> --Josh Billings

Be great in act, as you have
been in thought.
> --William Shakespeare

> **A life spent making mistakes is
> not only more honorable, but
> more useful than a life spent
> doing nothing.**
> **--George Bernard Shaw**

LIFE IS BUT A DREAM

Life is nothing more than a
dream. To some it may be a
nightmare. But if you don't
like the dream you are
living, you can change it.
Let me repeat this again.
Life is like a movie; if you
don't like what you are
seeing, change the script.
Rewrite it the way you want
to see it. A lot of people
don't like change, but change
is something that you have to
learn to embrace. Change is
good. Who wants to do the

same things all their life?
Who wants to have the same
amount of money all their
life? Who wants to live in
the same place all their
life? We need change. Life is
centered around change. Look
at the seasons: they change.
Look at time: it changes.
Your age changes. You are not
the same age you were last
year. Do you really believe
you can have the life you
want? The biggest problem we
have is that we are not
living our dreams; we are
living the dreams that we
have been told to believe.
The life you live now is not
your dream; it's somebody
else's dream that you have
been tricked into believing
is good for you. This world
we live in is an illusion. It
is not real. We were taught

from the moment we came out of the womb to believe the illusion of the world. What you haven't been told is how to create the life you want here and now.

THE POWER OF THE MIND

The mind is the most powerful weapon given to man. The most dangerous man in the world is a man that knows how to use his mind. Let's look at the conscious mind and the subconscious mind again.It is very important that you get this. There are two departments of the mind, the conscious and the subconscious. The conscious mind takes thoughts that you are thinking, whether they are good or bad, and gives them to the subconscious mind

to manifest. That is why it
is very important to control
your thoughts. Take your
dream and put it into your
mind and just think about
your dream. Your conscious
mind will take your dream to
your subconscious mind, and
the subconscious mind will
proceed to manifest it.
Understand that this will not
happen overnight. The more
you practice, the better the
results. Practice makes
perfect. One of the most
important dynamics of the
mind is raising your level of
consciousness because that's
how your dream becomes your
reality. You need to become
your dream. Whatever your
dream is, you need to become
one with it, as in a
marriage. Let no one or
nothing separate you from

your dream. I don't believe in working physically hard, but I do believe in working smart. Work your mind, not your behind. Have you seen people who work physically hard and are never happy, always tired, and feel like they are never fully compensated for their labor? They who use the unlimited powers of the mind are relaxing,playing golf,eating crackers,drinking tea and making a lot of money. While you are in the process of making your dream your reality, know that your mind is a magnet that will draw to it the things necessary to complete the mission. It was Albert Einstein who said that the imagination is more powerful than knowledge. In life we are taught that

knowledge is power, and it is
to a degree, but imagination
is the beginning of creation.

Those that use their
imagination are operating in
a whole different dimension.
That's why Albert Einstein
was considered a genius,
because he was at a level
where he used knowledge,
wisdom, understanding, and
his imagination. If you're
going to be successful in
making your dreams come true,
you have to be able to use
your imagination. One of the
secrets in playing the game
of life is that you have to
be able to create. Your mind
is powerful did you know that
you can heal yourself? You
can create money with the
power of the mind. When you
get to the higher levels of

mind power, you can even
manipulate your present
reality. When you come to a
dream block and can't find
what you need to make your
dream a reality, use your
imagination and create it.

DON'T TELL EVERYBODY YOUR DREAM

Everybody is not for you.
Everybody won't understand
your dream. Even if you
explain it to them, they
won't understand because they
are not supposed to understand; it's your dream. There
will be people who will be
jealous of you because you
are making your dreams come
true and they are not. These
people are the kind that will
try to sabotage your dream. I
call them "dream killers."

Your dream is like a baby
inside of you. It takes time
to develop before it's ready
to come out. It takes a
process. Don't try to rush
your dream for you don't want
it to come out premature. And
for God's sakes, don't abort
your dream. You need to align
yourself with other dreamers.
Get yourself around people
that are trying to do
something. Don't hang around
people who don't do anything.
You need to be around people
that will help you, not
become a problem. Your
friends are a future picture
of what you will become. Some
of the most important people
you have to deal with are
your family. If you are a
mother, your children and
husband won't understand you.
If you're a father, your

children and wife won't
understand. But encourage
them to support you and give
you the space and time to
complete the mission. Let
them know that at the end, it
will be worth it all. During
this time of turning your
dream into reality, you can't
forget your responsibilities.
It may get rough for a
period, but use your
imagination and create
solutions. Parents usually
want their kids to live their
dreams, but be careful, let
your kids live their own
dreams. Let them go for their
dreams. Sometimes parents can
crush a child's dream and not
even know it. When your
children come to you and tell
you about their dreams and
you think they are silly or
stupid, support and encourage

them. You won't understand
your child's dream and your
children won't understand
yours.

GO BACK AND GET YOUR DREAM

Life can hit us sometimes
with some hard blows and put
us in a position where we
have to make some serious
decisions. Many of us have
buried our dreams away
because we have had children
or we had to take care of our
parents, etc. Go back and get
your dream. It's not too
late. No matter what
circumstances you have to
deal with, you can still
bring your dream into
reality. Don't let your dream
die. A lot of people are not
happy; they just go through
life depressed, sad, and mad

because their life didn't turn out the way they wanted. They didn't pursue their dream. They got hoodwinked into believing the dream the world had for them. Everybody is born with a dream inside them. Your dream is still waiting to come out from where you buried it. The only thing that matters is bringing your dream into reality. Your dream will bring with it everything you need. You only get out of life what you are willing to get for yourself. Nice guys finish last. You have to learn how to be as wise as a serpent, as harmless as a dove.

CUT LOOSE YOUR ANCHORS

Manifesting your dream is like sailing onto big seashores, but in order to sail at a nice and steady pace, you have to cut loose your anchors. Your anchors can be low self-esteem, bad habits, hanging with the wrong people, also physiological wounds. These wounds can range from rapes, physical or mental abuse and domestic violence wounds that have not healed mentally, or emotionally. These are the worst anchors. They make it very hard to sail those great, big seashores to achieving your dream. Watch the company you keep. You don't need to be around

people who will hold you
back. Anchors are hard to cut
off. In order to complete
your dream, you need to be
able to navigate in many
different directions. If you
don't cut loose the anchors,
it will be extremely
difficult to get to the
finish line. Your family can
be an anchor. Put them on the
boat with you. Drugs are the
number one anchor you need to
stay away from. Not only will
they stop you from advancing,
they will also kill you. Make
sure that your mind is right
and that your health is right
because, while you are
sailing the sea of life, you
will run into some storms. If
you stay focused and
determined, you will make it.

I HAVE TO

Every dreamer has to have the attitude of "I have to." I have to make my dream come true. I have no other options but to make it happen. This is one of the most important components that dreamers need in their tool belts. With this kind of attitude, you will be amazed at how much you can accomplish. This is what I call the "marathon attitude" (I have to). When everybody is tired and stops, you still keep going until you get to the finish line and celebrate the victory that your dream has become a reality.

DON'T WORRY

You are not perfect. Nobody is. Worrying is something that cannot help you. Instead of worrying, you need to stay focused on your dream. You do not know everything. You're not supposed to know everything. Don't worry. Stay away from people that know everything. Nobody knows everything. You may not have all the resources you need, but don't let that get in the way of achieving your dream. You can not please everybody. No matter what you do, somebody is always going to have a problem with it. The dream you have is yours. The hell with them! People are going to talk about you and ridicule you. Your family and friends might not support you

the way you think they
should. You might not achieve
your dream in the time frame
that you had planned. Stay on
the path and don't give up.
Only the strong survive.
Don't worry, be happy!

GET OUT OF THE TRAP

Everybody knows that money
makes the world go round. In
order to live in this world,
you need money. Why? Nothing
is for free. You need a roof
over your head, food on your
table, and clothes on your
back. So you have to get a
job (trap) so you have money
to pay bills and survive as
any human being would. But
people like you and me want
nothing more than to manifest
our dreams. It takes a lot of
time and effort to achieve

your dream. It's hard when you have to work a 9 to 5 job that you hate but which pays the bills. To tell you the truth, we are not supposed to work for money; money should be working for us. That's how we got caught in the trap. You never stop having bills, or stop needing food, clothes, and shelter. So we continue to work to pay bills. You can't just get up one day and say you're not going to work any longer because you have responsibilities. You really don't like your job, but you have bills. You want to do so many things; you have some great dreams. Many people spend their entire life caught in the trap. Any time you are forced against your will to do something you

don't want to do and you keep
on doing it to survive, you,
my friend, are caught in the
trap. Who wants to live their
life working just to pay
bills?

I have a solution. You have
to work on your part time
dream until it becomes your
full time reality. Learn how
to become a money generator.
I believe in working your
mind, not your behind. If you
learn to create money in ways
other than by your 9 to 5
job, you can get out of the
trap. Go within yourself and
find ways to create money.
You will be free to do what
you want, when you want to.
Do not continue to be a
puppet and have someone
pulling your strings. Learn
how to pull your own strings.

Some of us have been in the trap for so long that it has become a way of life. Don't get me wrong. I'm not telling anyone to leave their job. But take what I am saying as food for thought. Maybe it's just me, but I don't believe life should be stressful and hard. But it should be happy, joyful, and great.

FREEDOM (FREE DOME)

There are a lot of people walking around who think they are free. Just because you are not in jail or in confinement, doesn't mean you're free. In order to be truly free, you have to free your mind. Your head is shaped like a dome; so in order to free yourself, you have to free your dome. Many of us are in the prison of our minds. We have been programmed with false information. Don't you see the mind is the most powerful weapon of man? You have to learn how to use your mind to create and control your reality. Free your dome and watch the chains fall off; and balance your freedom. No one can set you free but you.

When you free your dome, you are like the eagle that soars all over the world. As above, so below; as within, so without.

MANIFESTING THE DREAM

There are some very important components that you need when you are on your mission to manifesting your dream. These are the keys to unlock the doors of your dream.

1. **Knowledge**—The fact or state of knowing; clear and certain mental apprehension. The body of truths or facts accumulated in the course of time. Whatever your dream is, you need to be very knowledgeable about it. Get as much information as you can. Knowledge is power. We live in an information society. The internet is the source from which you

can get all the information you need. Find someone else who has done what you want to do. Maybe you can find out how they did it and use some of their tips.

2. **Wisdom**—The quality or state of being wise, sagacity, discernment, or insight. Wisdom is the ability to use the knowledge you have obtained the right way. You get wisdom from people who have done what you are trying to accomplish. By learning from their mistakes and success, you get wisdom, wisdom of what to do or what not to do. You need wisdom. Wisdom will save you a lot of heartache and grief.

Wisdom will help you make the best decisions on the road to unlocking the doors to your dreams.

3. **Understanding**—To comprehend the meaning and significance of understanding in achieving your dream. Knowledge and wisdom are nothing without understanding. Understanding helps you to make wise choices. Understanding will show you and help you unlock all the secrets of your dream.

4. **Passion**—A powerful emotion. The object of such enthusiasm. Passion is like a candle that must forever burn. Passion is a key element needed to

accomplish your dream. Passion will give you the endurance you will need on your journey. There are going to be some ups and downs and some difficulties, but if you're down and have passion, you might make it to the end. You have to keep that candle burning.

5. **Networking**—You have to get out there and make connections. Meet people who are doing what you want to do. Communication is the key. Learn how to mingle. You will always want to surround yourself with people who can help and who have knowledge, wisdom, understanding, and passion.

6. **Encouragement—** Encouragement is like oxygen to the soul. You have to encourage yourself even though there are going to be some rough times on your journey. Self-encouragement is what will be needed to keep you focused on the path. Encouragement can come in many different ways. It can come by music, movies, or anything that inspires you. Get a hold of it and don't let it go.

7. **The plan—**Write down your plan and strategy. Know what you want to do. Know how you want to do it. Know where you want to do it. Know when you want to do it. If you fail to plan, you plan to fail.

Plan for victory. Plan for success. When you are putting together your plan, always seek advice. Sometimes we get so caught up in the dream we forget about reality.

8. **Dream team**—You have to put together your team. Choose wisely. You need people to help you. You can't do it by yourself. You need people who are determined to help you accomplish your dream, people of like minds, people who are humble. You want to be around people who want to win in the game of life. One key to manifesting your dream is to help others achieve their dreams. One hand washes the other. You need

people who are good at
things that you are not.
You need people you can
trust.

9. **Meditation**—Find a quiet
   place where you can relax
   and not be interrupted.
   Close your eyes, take a
   deep breath, exhale. Go
   within, visualize your
   dream fulfilled, imagine
   that you're happy and
   joyful for achieving your
   goal. Visualize and
   imagine how it feels to
   have accomplished your
   dream. See yourself
   celebrating with your
   dream team. See yourself
   doing, being, and having
   whatever you want.
   Meditate every day. If you
   fail to go within, you

will learn to live
without.

10. **Maintaining the dream—**
After your dream becomes a
reality, that's when your
life begins. After a woman
carries a baby for nine
months, she gives birth
and she has to raise her
baby. The same with the
dream. After you give
birth to the dream, you
have to raise it and take
care of it. It will be
much harder to take care
of the dream than it was
to give birth to it. You
can do it because you will
do it. Get in the birth
position and deliver your
dream into the world.

LIFE IS BUT A DREAM

I am living the good life
I am doing what I love to
  do
I have everything I want
I can go anywhere I want
I have the biggest houses
I have the best cars

LIFE IS BUT A DREAM

I have the perfect life
No sickness
No danger
No stress
No heartache
Just love, peace and joy
I Have more money than the
  world has ever seen

LIFE IS BUT A DREAM

I have accomplished
  everything I wanted to

Everything I put my hand to
   do prospers
In my world there is no
   racism
No poverty
No low self-esteem
Only unity and strength

LIFE IS BUT A DREAM

Please do not wake me up!

I FOUND THE TRUTH

Everything that I thought was
   real was fake.
Everything that I thought was
   fake was real.

I FOUND THE TRUTH

Everything that I thought was
   right was wrong.

Everything that I thought was
  wrong was right.

      I FOUND THE TRUTH

Everything that I thought was
  good was bad.
Everything that I thought was
  bad was good.

      I FOUND THE TRUTH

  Open your eyes and see
  that the truth is right
  in front of you.
            --John 8:32

   I FOUND TRUTH, WHAT ABOUT
          YOU?

AFFIRMATIONS

My supply comes from God, and big happy financial surprises now come to me, under grace, in perfect ways now.

The unexpected happens, my seemingly impossible good comes to pass now.

As money goes out, immediately money comes in now.

Money comes to me suddenly in avalanches of abundance now.

I magnetize more and more money to me now.

All financial doors are open, all financial channels

are free as they now come to me.

Money, manifest thyself here and now in rich abundance.

I gave and it shall be given unto me good measure pressed down, shaken together and running over shall men give into my bosom. For with the same measure that I use, it will be measured to me again.

I am willing and obedient. I shall eat the good of the land.

I meditate on what I love, and I draw it to me here and now.

I am an unlimited person; I create my own world, here and now.

I meditate on abundance for myself as well as others, here and now.

I always have everything needed, here and now.

I magnetize peace, love, joy, well being, and happiness, here and now.

Good things come to me easily, here and now.

I trust and follow the God-in-me.

I am always in the right place at the right time, here and now.

I honor and praise myself in everything I do, here and now.

I allow myself to feel wealthy, successful, prosperous, and abundant, here and now.

I give myself permission to have what I want, to be what I want, and to do what I want, here and now.

I expect only the best to happen in my life, here and now.

All my solutions to all my problems are within me, here and now.

I always give my best. And the best is given back to me.

Everything is coming to me easily and effortlessly.

I have everything I need to enjoy my here and now.

I am the master of my life.

Everything I need is already within me.

Abundance is my natural state of being. I accept it now.

Every day I am growing more financially prosperous.

The light of God within me is producing perfect results in every phase of my life.

COMING SOON ...

I HAD A DREAM ABOUT HIP-HOP

GOSPEL MUSIC AT ITS BEST, VOL. I

THE BLUEPRINT

COSMIC CONNECTIONS

FAMILY AFFAIR

THE REAL WORLD

WATER WALKER RADIO

Contact Info:

Waterwalkerpublishing.com
Waterwalkerpublishing@yahoo.com